Taylor Swift
FEARLESS STAR

By Riley Brooks

D0368108

SCHOLASTIC INC.

New York   Toronto   London   Auckland
Sydney   Mexico City   New Delhi   Hong Kong

© 2010 by Scholastic
ISBN 978-0-545-30382-8

Published by Scholastic Inc.

12 11 10 9 8 7 6 5 4 3 2 1   10 11 12 13 14 15/0

Printed in the U.S.A.   40
First printing, November 2010

TABLE OF CONTENTS

INTRODUCTION

Have you ever wondered what it would be like to be a star? To sing your heart out in front of crowds of screaming fans? Release albums? Go on tour? Win tons of awards? It would be awesome, right?

Well Taylor Swift gets to do all of those things every day. These days Taylor is one of the biggest names in country *and* pop music. But before she was a singing sensation, she was just a regular girl from Pennsylvania.

CHAPTER 1 • FARM GIRL

Taylor was born on December 13, 1989. She grew up in Wyomissing, Pennsylvania. She lived with her parents, Scott and Andrea, and younger brother, Austin, on a Christmas tree farm. "I was raised on a little farm. . . it was the most magical, wonderful place in the world," Taylor told the *Ottawa Citizen*.

Taylor had a very happy childhood. She was always a natural at performing even then. "There

are videos of me walking up to strangers and singing songs from *The Lion King* when I was a baby," Taylor told the *Philadelphia Inquirer*. She was involved with her community's theater program. Taylor loved being on stage.

Taylor discovered country when she was six. She got a CD of LeAnn Rimes' album *Blue* and fell in love. "I knew every song she ever sang. . ." Taylor told gactv.com. Taylor knew then that she wanted to be the next big country star!

CHAPTER 2 • INTO THE SPOTLIGHT

Once Taylor decided to become a star, there was no stopping her. She began by performing at karaoke nights. She won lots of contests. She even won the chance to open for country stars when they performed in her town. From there, she started singing all over Pennsylvania. "Every single weekend, I would go to festivals and fairs and karaoke contests—any place I could get up

on stage," Taylor told cmt.com.

About a year later, Taylor decided to record her first demo CD. Then she and her mom drove to Nashville, Tennessee, the home of country music. Taylor went into every music label in Nashville and gave them her demo. Taylor didn't land a recording contract on that trip. But that just inspired her to work even harder.

Around that time, Taylor started junior high school. But a lot of her old friends didn't want to be friends with her anymore. Taylor was very hurt. She told the *Philadelphia Inquirer*, "It was a really lonely time in my life." Taylor's old friends were jealous of her singing success at fairs and in local singing contests. But that just made Taylor want to succeed more. She learned to play guitar. Then she started writing her own songs. "The thing that I found to escape from any pain. . . was writing songs," she told the *Toronto Star*. Taylor had a natural gift for songwriting.

Even though school was rough, Taylor's career was blossoming. Taylor caught the attention of a talent agent named Dan Dymtrow. Dan got right to work helping Taylor. When she was thirteen, Taylor recorded a new demo of her own songs. Dan took it to Nashville, and RCA, a country music label in Nashville, offered Taylor a development deal. That meant that RCA would pay for Taylor to work on some songs. Then they might release an album for her. Taylor was thrilled. But RCA was based in Nashville and the Swifts lived in Pennsylvania. So they packed their bags and moved down to Tennessee!

CHAPTER 3 • WELCOME TO MUSIC CITY

Taylor and her family moved to Hendersonville, Tennessee. That fall, Taylor started high school at Hendersonville High. She fit right in and made friends quickly. She met her best friend Abigail in English class. "We became best friends right away. . . we went through just about everything together," Taylor explained to gactv.com. Taylor also had her first boyfriend in

high school. His name was Brandon Borello. She wrote "Our Song" about him for her school talent show.

Taylor wasn't such a big hit at RCA. They wanted her to record music written by other people. But Taylor wanted to write her own songs. So after a year of work, Taylor walked away from her RCA deal.

Taylor shopped a new demo around town. A

label called Sony/ATV offered her a publishing deal as a house writer. Taylor was the youngest songwriter they had ever hired. Her job at Sony was to write songs—alone and with other writers. "I signed my publishing deal at age fourteen with Sony/ATV. I wrote a lot of songs. . ." Taylor explained to songwriteruniverse.com.

Taylor didn't try to write songs for adult singers. Instead she wrote about what she knew. She wrote about friendships, boys, and school. Taylor worked with a songwriter named Liz Rose once a week. Taylor would come in with ideas and Liz would help her perfect them.

Liz and Taylor wrote "Tim McGraw," Taylor's first big hit song together. It was about Taylor's then boyfriend who was about to leave for college. "I started thinking about all the things that I knew would remind him of me. Surprisingly, the first thing that came to mind was that my favorite country artist is Tim McGraw," Taylor explained to cmt.com. Liz also helped Taylor write several of her other singles. They wrote "Teardrops on My Guitar" about a boy named Drew Hardwick that Taylor had a crush on. They wrote "Picture to Burn" about an arrogant boy Taylor almost dated.

Taylor's songs caught the attention of Scott Borchetta. Scott started his own music label a few months later called Big Machine Records. Taylor was the first person he offered a record deal to.

CHAPTER 4 • BiG MACHiNE

Taylor got right to work for her new label. It took four months to record her album. They had decided "Tim McGraw" would be her first single. It was set to be released in June 2006.

In the meantime, Taylor decided to create a music profile for herself on MySpace. She wrote a fun biography and added pictures, video clips, the songs from her album, and her schedule for promotions. It was a great idea! Taylor's classmates became her first MySpace friends, but soon strangers were requesting to be her friend as well. People were listening to her music and loving it!

Taylor was so excited to have fans. She tried to respond to every e-mail they sent her. Lots of her fans had never listened to country before. They just loved Taylor's songs.

When "Tim McGraw" finally debuted, it was downloaded over 500,000 times in under five months. That was a big deal for an artist who had

never released a single before! A few weeks after "Tim McGraw" hit the airwaves, Taylor set off on a six-month tour to promote her album. She gave concerts, interviews at radio stations, and made special appearances. The rest of her singles raced up the country and pop music charts too! Her second single "Teardrops on My Guitar" went platinum. That meant that over one million people had downloaded her song! Then, Taylor's third single "Our Song" hit number one—it was her biggest hit yet!

In October, her self-titled debut album, *Taylor Swift*, finally made its way to store shelves. The album went platinum in under a year. "I can't comprehend that a million people are out there flying my flag and being awesome and buy-ing my record," Taylor told musiccitymoms.com. *Taylor Swift* went on to hit number one on the country charts and it eventually went triple plati-num. Taylor was officially a star!

Taylor worked very hard to make sure that her album stayed successful. She went on several tours with big country stars like Rascal Flatts, George Strait, Brad Paisley, Kenny Chesney, Tim McGraw and Faith Hill, Sugarland, Kellie Pickler, Alan Jackson, and many more! She was on the road so much that she got a custom tour bus in 2008. It's kept well stocked with all of Taylor's must-have items for the road. She always has lots of fun makeup, her cellphone, iPod, a laptop, her favorite guitar, and lots of pairs of cowboy boots.

Taylor also made special appearances on TV shows. She did thousands of radio interviews and signings in record stores. Taylor loved meeting her fans. She told cmt.com, "I'm still in the 'Oh-my-gosh-this-is-really-happening' phase. After all these concerts that I do, people line up and want me to sign things!"

One of the coolest album promotions Taylor got to do was making music videos for her singles. She made sure that her videos told a story. She also got to rock out with her guitar! But the best part of filming was getting to select cute boys to be her co-stars!

Taylor put out a few special albums for her fans before her big second album. The first was *Sounds of the Season: The Taylor Swift Holiday Collection* for Target stores. It was a Christmas album. The second was *Taylor Swift: Deluxe Limited Edition*. It featured all of the songs from *Taylor Swift* plus a few new songs, cool photos, and some videos! The third special album was *Beautiful Eyes* for Wal-Mart stores. All three albums made fans more excited for Taylor's next release.

CHAPTER 6 • FEARLESS

In 2008 Taylor recorded her second album, *Fearless*. A lot of songs were about love. "I'm very fascinated by boys and love and relationships. . ." Taylor told the *San Francisco Chronicle*.

Fearless hit store shelves on November 11, 2008. It instantly went to number one. It sold almost 600,000 copies in the first week! That's a lot of CDs! The album went platinum in 2009.

And eleven of its songs made the top 100 chart.

The success of *Fearless* opened a lot of doors for Taylor. She got to sing the National Anthem at the 2008 World Series. Then Taylor performed her single "Fifteen" with good friend Miley Cyrus at the Grammy Awards. She also made a guest appearance in Miley's *The Hannah Montana Movie*. But one of the coolest things Taylor did in 2009 was star in a video game! She became a character in the game Band Hero. These days, there are even Taylor Swift dolls. How cool is that?

Next, Taylor went on her fifty-two city *Fearless* tour. It was the first time that Taylor had been the star of a tour. She was very excited. So were her fans! Tickets for some locations sold out in under a minute! Taylor re-released a platinum edition of *Fearless* on October 27, 2009. It had six new songs, photos, a DVD of tour footage, and other behind-the-scenes goodies. Fans loved it!

CHAPTER 7 • THE AWARD GOES TO...

Taylor has only released two official albums but she's already won lots of awards. In 2007, she won the Country Music Television "Buckle Breakthrough Video of the Year" Award. Taylor told *The Tennessean*, "I can't explain the feeling. I had never been nominated for anything before. I had won nothing before, literally nothing. . . . When my name was called, I just ran up to the

stage at, like, one hundred miles an hour."

Then, Taylor won the Songwriter/Artist of the Year Award from the Nashville Songwriters Association International. Taylor was the youngest artist to ever win the award! Then, Taylor won the Horizon Award at the Country Music Association Awards. The Horizon Award is always given to a new country singer or group. And, to finish off the year, Taylor was nominated for a Grammy for Best New Artist. She didn't win but it was still a big honor.

In 2008 Taylor won "Top New Female Vocalist" at the Academy of Country Music Awards. She also won "Favorite Female Country Artist" at the American Music Awards. Then, at the CMT Music Awards, Taylor won "Female Video of the Year" and "Video of the Year." Next, she won "Favorite Breakout Artist" at the Teen Choice Awards.

In 2009 Taylor became the youngest art-

ist in history to win "Album of the Year" at the Academy of Country Music Awards. She also received the "Crystal Milestone Award" for Outstanding Achievement in Country Music. Taylor went on to win "Female Video of the Year" and "Video of the Year" for the second year in a row at the CMT Music Awards. She also won "Favorite Female Artist" and "Favorite Female Album" at the Teen Choice Awards.

At the 2009 MTV Video Music Awards, Taylor was nominated for "Best Female Video" for her single "You Belong With Me." She was up against superstar Beyoncé. But Taylor won. She was so excited. She was the first country artist to ever win a Video Music Award! But during her acceptance speech, Kanye West hopped on stage and grabbed the microphone from her hand. He told everyone in the audience that Beyoncé should have won. Taylor was really hurt. She didn't even finish her speech. Her fans in the audience, in-

cluding Beyoncé, were furious.

Beyoncé won the award for "Best Video of the Year" later in the evening. She invited Taylor back up onstage to finish her acceptance speech. "I thought it was so wonderful and gracious of her. . ." Taylor told starpulse.com.

It really hurt Taylor's feelings that Kanye acted like she didn't deserve to win. She would never do something like that to a fellow performer. Kanye apologized to Taylor after the VMAs. Luckily for him, Taylor was classy enough to forgive him. Now he can only hope she doesn't write a song about it!

By the end of 2009, Taylor had reached

some incredible milestones. In November, she set the record for the most songs on the Billboard Top 100 by a female artist at the same time with eight singles! Next she teamed up with Boys Like Girls to record the song "Two Is Better Than One," and with pop superstar John Mayer to record "Half of My Heart." Her fans loved hearing Taylor collaborate with other artists.

CHAPTER 8 • IN ON THE ACT

Taylor is well known for her musical talent, but she's also a great actress! In 2008, Taylor appeared in Brad Paisley's "Online" music video. She also filmed a super-cool documentary for MTV called *Once Upon a Prom*. In the documentary, Taylor picked a lucky high school boy, traveled to his town, and went to his prom with

him! Taylor's date was a huge Taylor Swift fan, so she made his dream come true! Taylor's best friend Abigail came along for the ride, too, and Taylor's fans loved getting to know her in the process.

In late 2008, Taylor appeared alongside the Jonas Brothers in their 3D concert film *Jonas Brothers: The 3D Concert Experience.* The movie premiered in February 2009 and was a huge hit with Jonas Brothers and Taylor Swift fans around the world. A month later, Taylor made her small-screen acting debut guest starring on CBS's *CSI: Crime Scene Investigation.* She gave an incredible performance, and her fans were amazed to see just what a great actress Taylor really is!

Folks in the acting industry took notice of Taylor's skills. She was asked to host *Saturday Night Live* in November 2009. Taylor was so excited! *SNL* has been on the air since the

1970's, and it's a huge honor to be asked to host the show. Taylor dove right into the experience and impressed the show's writers and cast with her willingness to let loose and try anything for a laugh. Taylor's show was one of the highest rated *SNL* episodes of the entire season. No one would be surprised if they asked her to come back and host another episode soon.

Finally, Taylor made her way to the silver

screen with a small role in the 2010 romantic comedy film *Valentine's Day*. She played a peppy high school cheerleader named Felicia opposite *Twilight* saga cutie Taylor Lautner.

CHAPTER 9 • 2010

As 2009 came to a close, Taylor discovered that she had had the most Top 40 singles for a female artist for the entire decade! *Fearless* was the best-selling album of the year, with more than 3.2 million copies sold. To top it off, Taylor's songs were played more than any other artists for the entire year on the radio and streamed the most online!

Every year gets better and better for country's sweetheart, so she was probably pretty excited as 2010 rolled around! At the start of 2010, Taylor released a new single called "Today Was a Fairytale" for the film *Valentine's Day*'s movie soundtrack. The song debuted at #2 on the Billboard Hot 100 chart and broke the record for first-week download sales by a female

artist. It was also Taylor's first #1 hit in Canada!

Of course, it wasn't too long in the new year that Taylor was itching to get back into the studio. She was eager to create a new album. After all, Taylor has been through a lot since her first album, and she wanted to share all of her ups and downs in new songs. "When I put out an album, I'd like to think that when people listen to that album it's like a diary of what I've been through in the last two years," Taylor told mtv.com. "So it's a really fun way to express how I feel and what I'm going through." Taylor recorded most of the songs in January 2010. She was so excited to be back in the studio that she brought in homemade cupcakes for her team to kick off the recording process. The much-anticipated album is set to release in October.

CHAPTER 10 • GIVING BACK

Taylor considers herself lucky. She gets to live her dreams every day, she's made lots of money, and she has a wonderful family who supports her. Of course, Taylor also knows that everyone isn't as lucky as she is. That's why Taylor has always made a point to give back to her community and fans. Early in her career, she was the face of a Tennessee campaign to help kids stay safe

online. She donates money regularly to the Red Cross to help them deal with disasters across the country.

She was especially thankful she had done so when Nashville was hit with a huge flood in May 2010. The Red Cross was one of the first organizations to help those who had lost their homes. Taylor was devastated when she realized how badly her adopted hometown had been hit. "It was the craziest thing that I've ever seen. I was at my house in Hendersonville, we were staring out the window, thinking it didn't seem like rain. It just seemed like something in a movie. It was really emotional for me because those are the streets I learned to drive on. People's houses are just ruined. It was so heartbreaking to see that in my town, the place that I call home, and the place that I feel most safe. I just send my love to my friends and neighbors who got hit harder than I did," Taylor told *Star* magazine. Taylor was

quick to help her fellow Nashvillites. She donated $500,000 to flood-relief efforts and performed with other country stars in a special concert "Nashville Rising: A Benefit Concert for Flood Recovery." Taylor's generosity went a long way toward helping Nashville recover from the flood.

Taylor has gotten involved in a number of other charities as well. Her favorites are those

that help children. She donated her pink pickup truck to the Victory Junction Gang, a children's charity in Nashville, and donated $250,000 to various schools across the country on her last birthday!

Her generosity doesn't end in America. Taylor even lends a helping hand to her fans abroad. She's donated money to the Australian Red Cross and $13,000 to Children in Need in the UK, as well as playing benefit shows in multiple countries. No wonder her fans look up to her so much—Taylor really is a hero!

CHAPTER 11 • GETTING PERSONAL

Taylor is a big star when she's at work. But at home, she's just a regular teenage girl. She loves watching TV shows like *CSI* and *Grey's Anatomy*, and eating junk food.

On breaks at home, Taylor hangs with her best Nashville friends, Abigail and fellow country star Kellie Pickler. She also loves spending time with her family. And whenever Taylor has a

stopover in Los Angeles she meets up with buds Selena Gomez and Miley Cyrus.

Last year, Taylor had been linked with actor Taylor Lautner, star of the *Twilight* saga movies. Fans thought they made a cute couple. Sadly, they were rumored to have broken up around her birthday in 2009. Maybe there will be a song about him on Taylor Swift's next album?

So what's next for Taylor? She plans to be around in country music for a long time, putting out albums and singing for her fans! She'd love to try her hand at more acting and hopes to continue working with other artists. Taylor loves writing her own songs and wants to write more songs for other artists in the future. No matter how her career blossoms, Taylor is always going to be successful. She has so much talent that the sky really is the limit for Taylor Swift.

JUST THE FACTS

TAYLOR SWIFT

FULL NAME: Taylor Alison Swift

BIRTH DATE: December 13, 1989

HOMETOWN: Wyomissing, Pennsylvania

CURRENT TOWN: Hendersonville, Tennessee

PARENTS: Scott and Andrea Swift

SIBLINGS: brother Austin

HEIGHT: 5' 11"

HOBBIES: songwriting, watching movies, boating

FAVORITE SONG: "Can't Tell Me Nothin'" by Tim McGraw

FAVORITE COLOR: white

FAVORITE FOOD: cheescake

FAVORITE HOLIDAY: Christmas

FAVORITE THING TO WRITE ABOUT: love!

LUCKY NUMBER: thirteen